COW

Copyright © 1993 Creative Editions.
123 South Broad Street, Mankato, MN 56001, USA
International copyrights reserved in all countries. No part of this book may
be reproduced in any form without written permission from the publisher.
Printed in Italy
Art Director: Rita Marshall
Book Design: Stephanie Blumenthal
Text Adapted and Edited from the French language by Kitty Benedict
Library of Congress Cataloging-in-Publication Data
Benedict, Kitty.
Cow/written by Andrienne Soutter-Perrot; adapted for the American reader
by Kitty Benedict; illustrated by Gérard Wuest.
Summary: An introduction to the cow's life cycle, digestion, and milk
production.
ISBN 1-56846-047-3
1. Dairy cattle—Juvenile literature. 2. Cows—Juvenile literature.
[1. Cows. 2. Dairy cattle.]
I. Soutter-Perrot, Andrienne. II. Wuest, Gérard, ill. III. Title.
SF208.B39   1992
636.2'142--dc20   92-14456

COW

WRITTEN BY

ANDRIENNE SOUTTER-PERROT

ILLUSTRATED BY

GÉRARD WUEST

CREATIVE EDITIONS

Many animals live on farms. Some are wild, like rats and mice, and some are domesticated, like horses, sheep, and cows.

A farmer may also keep birds, such as chickens, geese, and turkeys. Birds are animals that are covered with feathers and have two feet and two wings. Their young hatch from eggs.

Four-footed farm animals are mammals. Their skin is covered with hair or fur.

Cows are mammals, too. Like all mammals, their young grow inside the mother's body. After they are born, the mother feeds them with her milk.

WHAT DO COWS DO?

The cow is the biggest, heaviest, and strongest animal on the farm. Farmers raise dairy cows for their milk, and beef cattle for their meat.

A cow's milk is stored in her udder. The farmer milks the cow by squeezing her teats twice a day. Big farms use milking machines to draw the milk from the cows.

There are many kinds of cows, and they live in almost every country.
A cow's short-haired coat, or hide, can be black, white, red, brown,
or even spotted.

The cow's udder has four teats that the milk comes through. She
has a long, thin tail with a tuft of hair at the end.

A cow's foot has two toes that are protected by a thick, hard nail called á hoof.

A bull is a male cow that is kept for breeding. A steer is a male cow whose reproductive organs have been removed, making him calmer and easier to handle than a bull.

A baby cow is called a calf. For the first few months of its life, the calf drinks only its mother's milk. Then it is weaned from milk, and starts to eat grasses and grains.

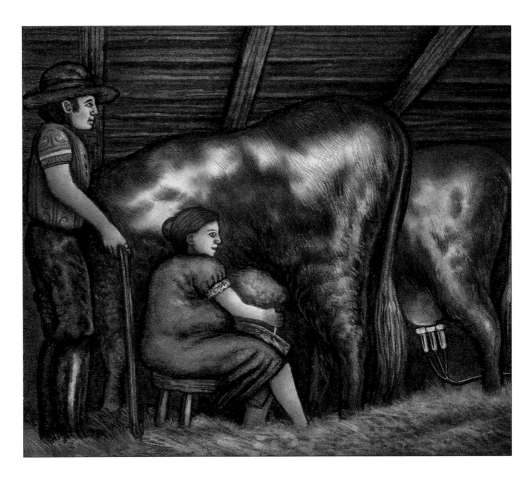

Even after her calf is weaned, the dairy cow continues to produce milk as long as the farmer keeps milking her.

A young female cow is called a heifer. She can be bred to have her own calf when she is about a year and a half old. Bulls start breeding when they are about a year old.

Nine months after breeding, the heifer gives birth to a calf. Then she begins to produce milk.

HOW DO COWS LIVE?

In the summer, cows eat fresh grass in the
pasture. In the winter, inside the barn, cows
eat dried grass or hay. Cows are herbivores,
which means they only eat plants.

A cow has special body parts to help her eat such coarse, tough food. First, she wraps her tongue around the grass and pulls it up, cutting it with her sharp lower teeth.

She swallows the grass all in a gulp, and it goes into a large pouch inside her body. This is her first stomach, also called the rumen. When this stomach feels full, the cow rests.

Small wads of grass are brought back up into the cow's mouth. She chews the grass with her large back teeth, back and forth, left to right. The cow is chewing her cud, or ruminating.

The well-crushed grass is swallowed once more. It goes into the
cow's three other stomachs, where it is broken down and digested.

Like all other animals, the cow uses the food she eats and the water she drinks to grow, move, and stay healthy.

The adult dairy cow also uses this food and water to produce milk.

WHAT DO COWS DO FOR US?

Cows grow strong and healthy in climates that are not too hot or too cold, and that receive plenty of rain to help the grass grow.

A good milk cow can produce as much as eight or nine gallons of milk each day. The farmer takes the milk to the processing plant, where it is pasteurized, or purified.

Milk is used to make cream, buttermilk, and many kinds of cheese.
We need milk and milk products in our diet.

Calves, heifers, steers, and old cows are sold to butchers for meat.

Cowhide is made into leather for belts and shoes. Cow horns and hooves are used for combs and buttons.

Even a cow's waste, or manure, is useful. It is taken out to the fields and used as fertilizer, which enriches the earth and feeds the crops.

No animal is more useful than the cow, since nothing it produces is wasted. In some parts of the world, the cow is even worshipped as a kind of god.